Voice at th
100
written ·   vn

elizabeth pike
02·11·20

by Elisabeth Pike

Dedication

This book is for everyone.

Everyone who is looking for the light in a hard time, everyone who is grieving, and anyone who is struggling in this strangest of seasons.

But it is most especially for Dougie and Siena, two rays of light who came into the world at this time.

ISBN 978-1-71673-524-0

Published by Little Bird Editions 2020.

About the Author

Elisabeth Pike lives in Shropshire with her husband and four children. She writes short stories, fiction and poetry and teaches creative writing. Her work has been published in The Guardian, Third Way, Fractured West, and in JUNO magazine amongst others. She sells her hand lettered poetry prints on her Etsy shop where she also takes commissions. *There You Are*, her book of 34 original hand-lettered poems about motherhood was published in 2017. She also writes on creativity and faith and her latest book *Circles: Nurture and Grow your Creative Gift* was released in April 2019. She has previously worked as a bookseller and librarian and has completed a Masters in Creative Writing from Goldsmiths University, London. She likes cities, long train journeys, and old photographs.

https://www.facebook.com/elisabethpikewriter
https://www.facebook.com/littlebirdeditions
https://www.instagram.com/elisabethpikewriter
https://www.instagram.com/littlebirdeditions
https://elisabethpike.tumblr.com
https://etsy.com/uk/shop/LittleBirdEditions

Voice at the Window:
100 gratitude poems written during lockdown

By Elisabeth Pike

Introduction

We will look back on this time with disbelief. I remember reading about the lockdown in Wuhan province, which began on January 23rd, 2020, where 500 million Chinese residents had to stay at home. No driving, no leaving the province, one trip out for groceries once every three days. Flights grounded. Factories closed. It didn't seem possible. At the beginning of this year I was working on a dystopian, post-Brexit novel. I didn't quite have the heart to carry on with it when I saw what was happening in the actual, real-life world. Lombardy, in Northern Italy, was totally overrun. There weren't enough intensive care beds or personal protective equipment (PPE). The pictures on the news looked like scenes from a disaster movie. Meanwhile, in the UK, we were waiting, anxiously. The Italians sang from their balconies in the midst of the pandemic though, and that gave us hope.

I am writing this on Wednesday 17th June and it isn't the end of the story. Non-essential shops have just opened up, and we are only allowed to meet in groups of six, outside. We are still very much in the middle of this pandemic. We still don't know how this will end, how many will die, when the children will go back to school, when (if) they will find a vaccine. But it seems like the world will be a very different place until then.

What else, I wonder, could stop the entire world in its tracks?

I started writing this series of poems on 26th February, my daughter's birthday and the first day of lent. I was struggling with winter blues and I thought that posting a gratitude poem on my social media accounts throughout lent would help me to focus on the positives. I didn't quite realise what we would all be living through a few weeks later. The poems seemed to resonate with people, and as I got to the end of lent, I was intending to stop posting, but a few people said, 'Please carry on!', and so I did.

In the end I stopped at #97 because a man named George Floyd was killed by a policeman in America, and it felt right to stop talking, and to listen. So, the last three poems have been added as afterthoughts. This isn't a political summary. This is my lived experience through lockdown. It's the strangest of things because although we have all been through this same thing, it has been different for all of us. Coronavirus still seems a distant threat to me. Almost like an urban legend, that you hear tales of, but that you never come face to face with. I haven't lost anyone close to me, but it has affected my life and the lives of everyone I know in a surreal but all-encompassing way.

I developed a routine that made me feel able to cope. The days were taken up with home school and after the kids were in bed, I would make a cup of tea, watch the daily update on iPlayer, and then type out a poem onto my notes on my iPhone. Each poem probably took half an hour to compose, although it's actually quite tricky editing on 'Notes' because you are deleting as you are typing. If a few spare minutes and an idea coincided during the day, then I jotted some ideas down in a notebook. In retrospect, this is a much easier way to compose poems as you can pick up the crossed-out scraps and put them to work again. I didn't miss a day, and I didn't actually find it hard, there seemed to be so much to say. I did sometimes have to post something that I wasn't entirely happy with, as I had run out of time but I'm not changing them too much now, just a few minor edits for ease of reading. The poems are what they are and they were formed under pressure, so I'm going to leave them as they are.

I did notice a difference in my happiness as I wrote these poems. Sure, some days were really hard and I felt like I was scraping the barrel for something good to write about. But looking for the positives

is refreshing because you start to see what is good and track it down, and then you realise that it is abounding all around you. All you have to do is look for it. I know this isn't new, it has been said over and over again. It's true though. And to quote one of my own lines, 'humanity's gift is this old earth, spinning on, with enough joy in each day to last for a lifetime, with enough beauty to keep us full to the brim with thankfulness. If you want to be full, look at the clouds, look into the eyes of others, look at the ferns, the birds, the sunset. Look and then keep looking for as long as you are alive.' (#46)
Thank you to everyone who liked, shared, commented on, or appreciated my poems. It means the world.

EP
x

[I have added the original comment that was shared with the poem on the day it was posted on social media in square brackets.]

(I have added editorial notes in round brackets.)

Gratitude #1

Thankful for the time when my baby naps,
even though I'm in a car park and this was not the plan.
She is meant to nap later, when I am at home and can work.
But instead, I am sitting in the car at Sainsbury's,
a ray of sunlight streaming in through the window.
Yesterday a precious friend came and made me brunch.
We laughed and talked. I felt loved and she was a ray of sunshine.
Later, my husband made me coffee and I cried,
just because it was a Tuesday and I think living in the country is
driving me crazy.
And then my baby girl danced on the sofa, wiggling her hips for the
first time.
And I thought I am so glad that you're here with us,
through all of the tears and stresses, I am so glad.
And today, my biggest girl is 9, and she is growing,
her heart becoming a tree of wisdom,
understanding more and more of this sad old world
as she grows.

26.02.20

[Going to do this for lent. A gratitude poem for each day. INSTEAD OF SCROLLING! X]

Gratitude #2

The sun breaking through the clouds,
the lightness that comes from the possibility of spring,
stable blood sugars, for today at least.
The floods are receding,
Tiny Leaves; the man and the music,
Nicholas Palmquist and his movements
that make me want to learn to dance.
Honesty and a cup of tea with a friend
that make me feel joined up, connected.

27.02.20

[It's noticing all the little things. And perhaps scrolling less which definitely affects my mental health negatively. Noticing what is good for us and what is bad for us. Self-care. Already feeling a bit lighter.]

Gratitude #3

I am thankful today
for the sound of a bird,
singing through the rain.
Thankful too for conversations with friends,
picking up where we left off,
sewing the story of our lives.
And for this day, for him,
the sum of three years' work,
a longing imagined and realised.
And then I see
how vast the possibilities -
for a lifetime.

28.02.20

[Even though it has rained all day, there are things to be thankful for! Even the rain.]

(Note: This was album release day for my husband Tiny Leaves, who had been working on his album 'Alone, not alone' for three years.)

Gratitude #4

Catching up with friends
over pizza.
A rainbow cake
made by Granny
to delight
my daughter.
Staying in the warm
while the storm rages
outside.

29.02.20

Gratitude #5

Thankful for my aching shoulders
because it means I have someone to carry.
Thankful for the calls of 'Mum'
because it means I am wanted.
Thankful for the pile of laundry on a Sunday night
because it means
we have had other things to do this weekend.
Thankful for this moment of quiet,
just now, where all I can hear
is the ringing absence of noise.
It echoes around the room,
or maybe it is in my head;
the first quiet I have known
in two days.

01.03.20

[Sometimes the niggles in our lives can be a source of annoyance, sometimes they can remind us of what we already have. My achy shoulders have been bugging me all weekend but there's a very good reason for that ache and it's called my one year old.]

Gratitude #6

Even though it is cold,
I am thankful
for the warmth of the sun
on my back
as I stand in the school field,
watching my daughter play football.
And this thought
comes back to mind,
a thought that has been thought
over eons, by millions of us.
That it is no small miracle
that the sun is neither too hot
nor too cold to sustain us;
that our small earth hangs
at just the right point in space to
receive all of its life-giving goodness.
That any change, however slight,
in temperature,
in degree of tilt,
in air composition
would have sent us
spinning off into space,
would have snatched life,
and all of these
infinite possibilities away.

02.03.20

Gratitude #7

Knowing that you will be writing about
gratitude sets your brain off
on a different track
from the moment you wake.
You are looking for the good things, not the bad,
and you roam through the day, taking notes.
You can pick almost-words, now,
from Annie's song; 'dabum', 'fsssh', 'light.'
You hear the throaty call of a crow in the sunshine.
You delight in the taste of a hazelnut latte with velvet foam,
from that independent café; the best you've tasted anywhere.
You wander in the sun with your husband and father-in-law,
talking of dreams and future things.
Later, your lovely Mum comes around
to do the dishes and play with Annie,
while you sit at your desk and write for one more hour,
finding another character who is opening up before you
and it delights your soul and your senses,
and you think,
I hope this gets somewhere
because I think I have something to say.

03.03.20

[Of course, there are bad things that happen every day and each of these days I could write a completely different poem but I am aiming to choose to see what is good and what I am thankful for in each day instead of raging about what makes me sad or angry!]

Gratitude #8

Today I am most thankful for the joy
of watching my firstborn play football
with his school team.
It lights him up like nothing else
and I am so glad that he has found
one of the things in his life that he loves.
I have been noticing the birds today;
how loudly they were singing
this morning, in the rain,
and now, as we cross the car park at 6pm,
and the sky is pink,
a blackbird sings its dusk song.
I wonder how many times a day
they lift the spirits of someone,
these feathered, singing friends.
I hope that there will always be a bird
singing somewhere,
not too far away,
to remind us that there is always
a song to be sung,
whatever is going on.

04.03.20

Gratitude #9

Today there are many things
and there is one thing.
I am thankful for this life
that I prayed for.
Tonight, after dinner,
we tidy her toys to play a game,
and there is a moment
when her whole family is
surrounding her in a circle,
and we start to copy whatever
she does. We wiggle our legs,
raise our hands up in the air,
shake our heads from side to side,
just as she does, and her eyes light up
when she realises the power that she has.
It is one of those moments
that is perfect in its beauty
and its silliness,
and I hope that we remember it,
and I see again what an honour it is
to watch you emerge,
little butterfly.

05.03.20

[All about one of the loves of my life, little Annie Mae]

Gratitude #10

Tonight we go out to a restaurant.
You, me and the waiter
are the only ones there.
We talk by the light of a candle
and I sit close to the radiator.
The food is delicious
and we eat until we are full.
We are getting older,
and it sometimes feels like time
is running out;
there is still so much we want to do.
It feels like a long time ago
that we met and fell in love.
It was here, though,
in this same town.
Maybe not so much has changed.

06.03.20

Gratitude #11

There is something to be said
for just finishing the cup of tea
while it is still hot,
for using the best hour
of the evening
to get a few more words
on the page
before you are too tired,
before you had better
finish off the dishes
and get the laundry done.
There is something to be said
for just having a moment
to sit and write a poem,
because there will always
be jobs to do,
and things will be done
as they must,
but there are some things
that are worth more
than a clean house;
to me, anyways;
Finding the peace
that brings me back to me,
that anchors me to the ground.
Finding my voice,
and getting it on that page.

07.03.20

Gratitude #12

Everywhere I look there are buds.
Even on the branches that have been swept clear
of the trees by winds or flood, they are still trying to live.
These orphaned branches are a little sad;
how covered in buds they are,
how much life they had to give.
But new trees can grow, can't they,
from a felled branch? I'm sure I've seen it.
And really, is anything impossible out here, in the woods,
where there are no humans to set the rules, to fix things?
Out here, growth wins.
Wild striving is the only thing that works.
There is a determination to grow,
to thrive even, against all odds;
even when life has been chopped at the stem.
Out here there are miracles that no one even sees.

08.03.20

[This one's a rough sketch! Lots of ideas, doesn't quite feel fully formed, but I've run out of time today. I just love seeing the buds at this time of year – they give me such hope. Renewal, growth, making new, tiny beginnings, all the good stuff!]

Gratitude #13

For walking out of old things into new things.
For a walk with my friends around Attingham,
for my sweet poorly daughter and my creamy latte.
For watching football in the rain,
for that phone call,
for the hour and a half waiting at gym,
when I got to finish my book
all about that other world
behind the Berlin Wall.
For Annie and that twinkle in her eye
at bedtime that said,
I can nearly stand on my own and I know it.
For my crazy children,
talking at me one hundred miles an hour,
telling me stories of their day
when they should be getting into bed.
For anchovy pasta, our go-to dish
when we have no time
and the cupboards are bare.
It is salty and rich and
we sigh with relief when we taste it.
It means the day is done and we can rest.

09.03.20

(Note: 'that phone call' refers to some progress with the house move. The book about the Berlin Wall is 'Stasiland' by Anna Funder – a fascinating read, and the pasta dish is taken from Diana Henry's fantastic book, 'Crazy Water, Pickled Lemons'.)

Gratitude #14

Thinking of what Annie Dillard said,
that you don't so much as write a book,
but sit up with it. And this is where I am now,
sitting with these two characters and wondering
why their relationship has fallen apart,
on what axis it will spin,
and how its fallout will affect the others.
I think it wonderful and absurd,
that this is how I have chosen to spend my life,
to suspend these imagined people with my words,
to illustrate birds, migration, being outside, being in.

Later, I am jolted into the real world,
where people wander around Sainsbury's
with mistrust in their eyes.
We are all quietly scared of this outsider; this virus.
Mostly though, we are good mannered
and there is not so much panic buying as you might have thought.
A man leans over and says 'plums', to the shop assistant
with a serious look on his face
and I can't stop smiling and thinking
how hilarious we humans are,
and also, that it is the basic belief
in people's goodness
that makes this world spin.

10.03.20

(Note: Annie Dillard said this in 'The Writing Life', which I highly recommend.)

Gratitude #15

It is the sun today
that I am thankful for.
It warms, it heals.
I take Annie to town
to look for a present for my dad,
and I realise what a pretty place it is,
with the river winding around,
the blue sky and the sunlight
falling around the street corners.
It still doesn't feel like my town though, -
funny since I've lived here
for 24 of my 37 years.
I read something that Toni Morrison said,
that when we realise when we don't
feel at home anywhere,
it is because we are at home everywhere,
and that is our new truth.
Funny, how I have spent so long
wondering where my home is.

11.03.20

[All about the sun and home.]

Gratitude #16

Instead of fear,
tonight, I am thankful
beyond measure
for creativity,
for this group of strangers,
united by their love for God,
their need to create.
And here we sit,
drinking coffee as the
wind rages outside,
picking apart how we create
and why,
and what does it mean?
And it literally makes me
want to cry
or shout 'YES!'
from the depths of myself.
This is what it is all about.
All of it.

12.03.20

[Earlier today, I listened to Boris saying that we could lose loved ones and felt a pang of despair. And yes, these are scary times. But we have to say no to fear, just keep going, wash our hands and be sensible. And then we went out to our CCN meeting (Christian Creative Network) and I came back buzzing with the truth of two amazing artists – their journeys and the truths they have learned to tell with their whole lives.]

(Note: This is the last time that my husband and I went out alone. It was also my dad's birthday and we quickly exchanged presents before they babysat for us- also the last time they were in our house and the last time they were allowed to babysit!)

Gratitude #17

I think it could become a habit,
this thankfulness.
And actually, in such uncertain times
as these, isn't it all about being thankful
for the moment that we are in,
really listening to the sounds we can hear,
savouring the things we can taste,
looking for peace in the moment?
I sit in a coffee shop window,
watching the walkers go by
in this strangely quiet town,
and wonder when it will all be done,
and when we will be able to walk out again
without worry, meet in public,
fly like birds,
unconcerned with borders.

13.03.20

(Note: this was the last day I did anything 'normal'. It was Friday 13th March and I went into town and had a haircut while Joel looked after Annie, then I met a friend for a coffee.)

Gratitude #18

Such a strange day.
Not reading the news, reading the news.
Not feeling fear in my heart, feeling overwhelmed.
But what can we actually do
except to be careful, stay home,
wash our hands, and hope that this will pass?
We can refuse to give in to fear
and stop scrolling news stories,
because our brains were not
built to take in so much bad news.
So I'm switching off, staying local,
looking after my little ones,
weathering this storm,
just as soon as the last has passed.
Longing for summer already, a clear head,
a new house, an end to this virus.
The children want to make cakes
from their school cookbook,
and we end up with cookies and carrot cake
for pudding which is alright by me.
When it all feels a bit too much,
and you don't know what lies
on the road ahead, at least there is cake.

14.3.20

[Not the most gratitude-y of poems today. Everything is a bit unknown. But all we can do is all we can do. And then we just have to hope that this will all pass like a bad storm and dream of the summer where we will be warm and go for walks by the sea.]

Gratitude #19

I wake this morning
and hear the soft coo
of the wood pigeon
and hear the blackbirds sing.
The earth is warming up
and it feels that we should be
breathing a sigh of relief
now that we have made it through winter!
But instead, the virus of fear is spreading,
faster, even, than the virus itself.
But the earth knows nothing of this;
it is readying itself for growth,
for spring,
for summer,
for life,
and it is 'tutto andra bene',
that the Italians are singing
from their windows;
'All will be well'.

15.03.20

['All will be well'. This shall all pass. Sending love and peace to everyone today.]

Gratitude #20

Today I am thankful for faith,
which always looks for hope.
I am thankful for the sun,
for birdsong,
for the earth coming to life again.
I am thankful for our NHS,
our government,
our nation.
I trust them, for once,
and feel safe on this island.
I am thankful for this girl,
doing new things day after day,
crawling in the garden,
feeling the damp dark mud
under her fingers,
kneeling up and bouncing
on the trampoline,
holding a black pen
and putting it to paper,
delighted in the marks she is making.

16.03.20

[We're on lockdown. Ben had a temperature on the weekend so that's us now, self-isolating for 14 days! The good things are a) I don't mind being in! b) Ben's symptoms were very mild so if it was CV and the others get it, it hopefully won't be too bad. c) One of my husband's gifts is working as a teacher so he has drawn up a timetable for the kids to follow. It includes exercise and packing as well as English and Maths! We're moving house in two weeks (in theory!!)]

(Note: In retrospect, this trust was probably misplaced. Experts have said that our country entered lockdown too late and if it had been even a week earlier, the death toll may have been halved. Ben stayed off school due to his temperature and Ivy and Sam went as normal following the advice.)

Gratitude #21

My sharp little children like fidgeting squirrels
as they try to work from home today,
pinging up from their seats every two minutes with a question;
'Mum, what does precious mean?',
'Where is the equator?', 'How do you spell prove?'
And I wonder how do teachers do this, every day, with 30 kids.
I almost forget to post today because I am watching the news,
but at least they aren't telling us how many people have died,
well not emphatically. They are stemming the hysteria.
There is the mental health of the nation to think about,
there is carrying on with it, there is the almost total removal
of all that is normal for the time being.
I doubt it will need repeating but I am thankful today
for the warmth of the sun on my skin.
Funny that it has come under these circumstances;
one fight breaks, another starts.
I don't want to know how many people have died today,
I want to know how many laughed until they cried
at the quality of their home-schooling,
and how many did something utterly new for the first time.
I want to know how many have done something good today;
bought someone shopping or sent them a text.
I want to know how many have talked to loved ones
on FaceTime or WhatsApp.
Thankful now for the technology that I railed against in winter
for keeping me depressed and alone, and now, in spring, this crazy
spring,
we can talk to Granny, Grandad, Mum and Dad, who we otherwise
couldn't see.
Thankful for the teachers, bringing work to our front door,
doing everything they can at a time like this.

Thankful for all the heroes who are saying, 'I can do something' and doing it.
Thankful for Grandad posting boxes of Shreddies through our window.
Thankful for the wine and chocolate delivered by Hannah when we asked for frozen mince.
There is a whole lot of good in this world people, a whole lot.

17.03.20

(Note: This was our first day of lockdown, Tuesday 17th March. Ben had a temperature on the evening of Friday 13th March and had been off school on Monday. On the evening of Monday 16th March, Boris Johnson asked the whole household of anyone who had had a temperature or a new persistent cough to self-isolate for two weeks. So we began lockdown a little earlier than everyone else. The fight referred to is my struggle with winter.)

Gratitude #22

Thankful today for my Yorkshire puddings,
blooming in the oven like little golden clouds.
They have never worked before.
Thankful for the hour in which
I could peel carrots, parsnip, swede
and put the chicken in the oven in silence,
while Joel took the children to the field,
to let off some steam,
to expend their energy.
Silence has always been my home, my rest.
I just chose to fill it
with all these little shouting bodies
(myself included).
We are full of nervous energy today.
I am tetchy, tired, on edge.
But children are children;
they do not look at the big picture,
they look at the now.
I show Ben the biscuit selection and he shouts out,
'This is the worst day of my life!'
I ask, 'Do you want to put some chocolate spread
on that biscuit?', and he replies with glee,
'This is the best day of my life!'
Thankful for my little boy,
for the wisdom of the now,
for the switch from gloom to joy, immediately,
for the sake of the taste of chocolate spread
on his tongue.

18.03.20

[Had to dig deep for this one today. There are always little things to be thankful for. And even if they seem small cast against the grey mass of CV which seems to loom over us, the truth is that this shall pass, and things shall go back to how they were before, but maybe they will be even better, because we will have reassessed all that really matters in life.]

Gratitude #23

Today, I am amazed at how the world has been turned upside down,
how people have been asked to undo their understanding of how to
live,
to reinvent, overnight, the way that they make money and see their
friends.
Pushed backwards into their homes,
they are still burning with the need to connect, to help, to see, to love.
Beautiful light bulbs shining all over this tiny, huge world.
And so they give. All of these exercise instructors, artists, musicians,
writers.
They give what they do for free, because it might help someone.
This beautiful internet has really joined us at the hip hasn't it?
We are one and the same, flesh and bone, vulnerable bodies
but fierce souls, burning with passion in this dark night.
Do we have it in us to stay in, to cut ourselves off, to stem the tide of
this thing?
Annie, my one-year-old, pushes her face into my cheekbones,
rolling her body up close to mine tonight, so she can sleep.
We are one and the same, together and apart, in love all the same.

19.03.20

*[Too much to say today, the line breaks had to go! Keep going GB, stay in as much as
you can. It's not forever and it's what will turn this thing around.]*

Gratitude #24

Thankful for my children's school, where the teachers work tirelessly
and this week have been racing against time, against this shock.
Thankful for the blue skies today, on the Shropshire hills.
We drive to a remote spot where we can't see a single other soul
and the children run around on the mossy grass, in the freezing wind.
Thankful for Shrewsbury, this town with its cobbled streets and its
wide, green river.
It has been a cruel year, first the floods and now this,
and so many businesses have had to bend and flex against the
pressure.
And now, these weird and wonderful eateries are doing takeout
and I pray for divine inspiration for the entrepreneurs of this town,
that they would be able to keep going in some way.
I am sure there is a way through this,
if we bend and sway,
and life will come back to life,
again.

20.03.20

*[I hope these poems aren't coming across as glib. I know this is such a difficult time, for
so many entrepreneurs especially, who are seeing a drastic change in their income and
livelihood. Shrewsbury is a real hub for entrepreneurs and small businesses so support
them as much as you can if you're local (loads of amazing restaurants offering takeaway
at the mo). I am mostly a stay at home mum with my one-year-old at the moment and I
squeeze my writing in wherever I can. But my income as a writer and a hand-letterer
has always been secondary so the shock for me is cushioned in that I spend a lot of my
time at home anyway and also I can continue both of these income streams at home (if the
kids will let me!). My husband is a musician and part-time lecturer in a college so he's
not too worried about future income at the moment. But for everyone around us, this
season is life-changing. It reminds me of when Ivy (my 9-year-old) was diagnosed with
Type 1 diabetes and we thought, 'How will we even get through an hour? How will we*

get through a day? How will life ever get back to normal?' And to be fair it hasn't ever gone back to 'normal' and, likewise, I don't think we will go back to normal because this will change and shape all of our lives but there is still joy and thankfulness to be found on the other side, and all the way through this scary time, if we look for it.]

Gratitude #25

Thankful for this house today,
the one that has guided us from one life into the next.
Last time we moved, we were young and
it felt that everything was still before us.
And now, 6 and a half years later, I feel old.
My face has changed and my heart has too.
It was here, in this old house that we sat down,
eight weeks after moving,
six weeks after Benjamin arrived,
with our sorrows,
with broken hearts for our daughter,
newly diagnosed with Type 1 diabetes.
It was here that our life was undone
and built up again from scratch.
It was here that I made two books,
and watched my children grow
into these strange and beautiful beings,
utterly set apart from me.
They are completely their own.
It is here that I have laughed many times and cried many tears.
It is here that my husband has written his way
into the clouds in his Shedio.
Farewell dear house, old friend.
Thank you for being our shelter in the storm,
and our garden in the spring.

21.03.20

[Our house. (I make no apologies for completely ignoring what is happening in the world at the moment, just homing in today.) We moved here six and a half years ago, and then it felt a bit like our lives fell apart when Ivy was diagnosed with T1 diabetes, but we got

*back up and kept on going but her diagnosis has certainly changed me from the core...
But anyways, I wanted to talk about the house! We moved here as it was the only 3 bed
house to rent at the time in the village. By the time we had exchanged on our house in
Guildford, I was heavily pregnant so didn't want to make the trip up to Shropshire so my
Mum and Dad came to view it. They said they would happily live here and so that was
that. We moved in without ever having seen it. And it has been such a surprise of a
house to us. The garden has these little secrets that come out throughout the year; the
primroses and crocuses that pop up through the lawn in March, the cherry blossom that
floods the tree in April and May, the cascade of roses on the trellis in June, the unfurling
ferns, the deep red of the Cherry tree in autumn, the red rosehips and pears. Thinking
about it, I will miss it quite a lot! But it is time for us to move on, to a place of our
own, up on a hill with a view. It feels like a writer's house and I can't wait!]*

(Note: the Shedio is my husband's affectionate name for his studio in the garden.)

Gratitude #26

I always thought I had to escape this place;
this town, my home, my parents,
but then I realised at a certain point, that I felt rootless
wherever else I lived.
And then one day, we came back, and began again.
And it feels like this to be back here: safe, known, loved.
Thank you, Mum, for your friendship,
thank you for loving our children as if they were your own.
Thank you for praying for us, supporting us, looking after us, still.
Every time I try to write it down, my words seem so small,
inadequate somehow, because your love is fierce and wide.
The children make me cards today,
I look at Annie's, and it reminds me of this poem;
the beginnings of meaning, so much more to say.

22.03.20

[I love my Mum to bits and today I am thankful for her. I find it so hard to put into words what she means to me. But here is a start.]

(Note: Mother's Day)

Gratitude #27

Is it ok to be thankful for my life today?
to be thankful for all that I have here in this garden in the sun,
to forget all that is going on outside these hedges,
to pretend that it is just a sunny day,
and we are just hanging out in the garden?
Is it ok to be thankful for children who distract me and keep me so busy
that I don't really think about the virus today?
I think instead about what I can cook
with the food that we have left,
how we will pack the rest of the house up in three days,
if we will be able to move, and how funny Annie is,
bouncing on the trampoline, her hair full of static.
Is it ok to be thankful for their fights, that keep this all so normal?
If they are anxious, they hide it well.
It is me and their Dad that try hard not to read news reports all day,
and then see a headline that we can't forget.
Why do you look at your phone all the time, she says at bedtime,
and I think because I want to distract myself
by watching something completely stupid,
completely unimportant, and at the same time,
I scroll past a post about someone's father dying.
Is it ok that the kids had a very long lunch break today
and then a long afternoon break
because it feels wrong to be inside
when the earth is inviting us out into its warmth?
The garden is a state, the boys have turned the grass into a football pitch
and it's too late to try to rescue any of it,
but I lie with my girls on the trampoline and look at the blue sky,
the silken clouds, and I think if this was any other spring,

if this was any other March, we would just be saying, 'How beautiful!'
My heart is not quite ready for this.
It feels like a trauma today,
a deep sadness that I have been trying to keep at bay.

23.03.20

[This poem ain't gonna make anyone feel very happy sorry!]

Gratitude #28

Sitting here with the debris of the day scattered about,
and piles of cardboard boxes stacked up against the sofa,
I have the feeling that we are drifting out to sea.
It's not just us and this move, this whole world is at sea.
We are undoing this life as we knew it,
and bundling it up into boxes,
and we will remake it in another place.
And it is the same for all of us, isn't it?
We have all packed up our lives and are entering this strange time,
this in between time: at sea.
We don't know how long this will go on for,
or what it will be like when we reach dry land.
Everything is stripped away except for 'don't get ill',
and 'don't make anyone else ill', and also 'love one another'.
And all of us, in this unknown place, are clinging on to all that is good.
My most precious things are right here with me, wrapped up on this
raft.
And it seems all we can do is hang on until we get back to shore,
and then we'll see where we are, what it is like in this new place,
and we'll take it one day at a time.

24.03.20

[Thankful for my little bundles with me on the raft! The longer this goes on, the more it feels like this is causing a seismic shift in our society, that it is changing our lives forever, that there will always be a before and after. But maybe that's not such a bad thing.]

Gratitude #29

We go for a walk around the village,
for our daily exercise,
and end up at the football field,
where the children
kick a football around for a while.
Sometimes all of this feels quite normal,
except for the part where you cross the street
if someone is coming towards you.
There are two moments of quiet today,
when I realise I am thankful.
A cup of tea in the garden
in the morning where I can
smell the earth
warming up around me,
And later at the football field,
where I breathe in as deep as I can
and can feel the sweetness
of the grass in my lungs.

25.03.20

Gratitude #30

Thankful for all the memories good and bad, in this home.
It's too hard to remember all the things that have happened here,
I am up too close.
In a little while, I'll look back
and see what it meant to us, what it taught us, how it changed us.
We moved in with a three-year-old, a two-year-old
and a two-week-old,
and we're moving out with a ten-year-old, a nine-year-old,
a six-year-old and a one-year-old.
We were different people when we moved in;
younger, looking for the next step.
We didn't realise this one would take so long
and have lived impermanently here.
We have had the same floral curtains up in our bedroom
that were here when we moved in.
We were reticent to paint, not knowing how long we'd be staying.
We have had a diabetes diagnosis here,
I had a baby here, we have made albums and books here.
And now we leave but say thank you to this old house,
to all that it has given us
and all the whispers of things past that have journeyed with us.
Strange to think of all that has gone before in this house,
the births and deaths.
Strange to think that we are moving to a place
that I would have never thought about living in,
to a house that is not built in a style I have ever dreamed of,
but could be everything we have been waiting for.
And who knows what secrets the new place will reveal,
or what will unfold in us as we live there?
Such a long time we have waited for this,
and now it is upon us

and I almost don't feel ready,
distracted by everything else that this year is throwing at us.

26.03.20

[Farewell to our lovely old house]

Gratitude #31

We're here, at last,
in the new house,
and it feels light
and full of peace
and it is everything
that we were waiting for.

27.03.20

[We're in! It is so light and beautiful here. Up on a hill. It's a bungalow (curve ball for me who has always dreamed of a Victorian terrace) and there is a view to die for. Tired now so today's poem is short and sweet!]

Gratitude #32

It's easy to think of things to be thankful for today,
even though there is tiredness,
and there are arguments, inevitably.
There is the light on the sheep in the field at breakfast time,
the way that the clouds light up as the sun moves across the sky,
and the way that the pink glow lingers
in the corner bedroom at seven.
We ring for a delivery of groceries,
and a couple of hours later, it is there at our door.
We eat a lunch of good ham, bread and salad.
Ham feels like a luxury, we haven't had any for a week.
We are thankful to our Mums for deliveries of dinner
two nights in a row.
We feel wrapped up in love up here.

28.03.20

Gratitude #33

Thankful in between the tiredness today.
We are overwhelmed by how much there is to do,
by all the things we have gathered over the years,
and are sorting and categorising all day.
The boys do not understand helping to unpack,
and ignore their bedroom, full to the brim with boxes
and run outside to play football.
We squeeze our pine dining table into the kitchen
and sit at it at dinner time,
looking out at the Lawley basking in the sun.
All of us have thankful hearts.
The children are suddenly interested in stories from my life,
like the time in Reunion, where we didn't eat breakfast
and then went on a hike through the forest
and then for a swim in a plunge pool
and my face went green because I had low blood sugar,
and the time I fainted at a gig with Ben in my tummy.
They retell the stories to me, as if they have always been here in my
life.
We have no internet and the children are bored,
while we go from one task to the next, from morning to night.

29.03.20

Gratitude #34

Thankful for this moment, right now,
where I can eat this creme egg and drink this tea in peace.
The children are finally all asleep and I have just sat down.
It is 9.15pm.
We still haven't finished emptying the old house,
but we don't go back today, there's too much to do here.
Decision making is tiring work, but it is what we have done all day.
We will find peace here but it will take time for the dust to settle.
I'm still not sure where my writing corner will be
although there is a shed in the garden that looks just right.
It's funny, being uprooted in spring.
It's the wrong time of year isn't it, to move things?
It is when plants awaken, take hold of the earth and unfurl;
they don't like to be moved then.
For me too, spring has always been a dance of creativity,
I have always revelled in the warmer days of March,
April and May, the sun on my face, the words in my hands.
But this year, I can't write, not yet. It will take a while.
There is too much tiredness in my bones,
too much noise in my head, too much illness in the world.
We were so ready to be uprooted, to be here,
but getting back to ourselves, our art, our work, feels like wading
through a room filled with paper and trying to get to the other side.
We go out wandering today, working ourselves into our new
surroundings, into the landscape.
We say we won't move again and that this is it now, this is us.
But it still feels the Earth has shifted under our feet,
and that when we emerge from this, everything will be different,
illuminated by thankfulness, gratitude, joy, perhaps.

30.03.20

Gratitude #35

Good things can come from this.
There is time now to cook a meal
each night at dinner,
for one of the kids to help out,
for us to go for a walk together after we eat.
There is time to help the children
tidy their rooms before bedtime.
In a normal week, before all of this,
we had gymnastics and football on a Monday,
swimming on a Tuesday, gymnastics on a Wednesday,
and football on Saturday and Sunday too.
There was never time to eat together.
We were always rushing,
handing over the baby
with vague instructions
as to what to cook for the kids
and what else needed to be done.
This thing, this pause
is a reset button in our lives.
It says,
'This is what you need.
This is essential.
This will help you live'.

31.03.20

Gratitude #36

Sam and I go exploring
in the wasteland behind the house.
We scramble up a steep bank;
a part of the Iron Age hill fort,
that was there long before us.
Funny to think of our house,
nestled in at the bottom of its ridge,
of those ancient humans,
and of our lives, following on,
overlaid in this place.
What remains in the land
and what is passed on?
What happened here? -
what battles, what births?
They too, would have stood
on this bank and looked out as we do.
Sam takes out his metal detector, hopefully,
but finds nothing today.
I am thankful today, for this land,
for all that has gone before,
and I say a prayer for anyone
who is suffering today,
because cut off as we are,
in this new house with no internet,
we are all sisters and brothers in this.
There is no life,
but that we are in this all together,
no breath
but the air that we breathe is all the same.

01.04.20

Gratitude #37

There is warm sun today so we relax in the garden for a while,
not holding our backs up against the chill.
Annie is learning to say no, whilst waggling her finger.
Amazing to think of her little self, emerging day by day.
My eldest daughter makes cookies,
and then lands a back somersault on the lawn, to squeals of delight.
My eldest son has found the balance of football to home-school
and sits down tonight in happy exhaustion,
in his natural state; grubby and tired.
My littlest boy has been drawing a book about Easter
and then helping his dad cut down a bush
to make room for the trampoline.
This is perhaps the biggest change for him, I think,
who has only known one house for most of his six years.
He is learning resilience and gentleness at once.
Tonight at 8, we step outside to hear the whoops and cheers for the
NHS
and I think I hope they know how thankful we are,
even if it is touching us only distantly at present, it is still touching us.
The sheep and the birds join in with the hoots and hollers.
Almost as if they know what is going on too.

02.04.20

Gratitude #38

Thankful for an early morning
with Annie, eating Shreddies.
Thankful for the sun always.
Thankful for a walk around the village.
Thankful for roast chicken for tea.
Thankful for a free stream of
Joseph and his Technicolour Dreamcoat,
I have always loved the story of the dreamer.
Thankful for the coming weekend
where we will stay inside, stay in our garden,
unmuddling this mess, all these things
that have silted up over the years,
all these things that we thought we needed,
that now, in this new house,
we see we didn't need at all.
Thankful that this storm will pass,
Thankful for the NHS, for these workers,
these lovers who give out their care
at great expense to themselves.
My offering, these words on this page,
seems frugal by comparison,
but it's what I was given to give.

03.04.20

[Sometimes it can feel like we don't have a lot to offer to the world, and in the face of a crisis like this, we can say, 'What can I do?', 'How can I help?' Well the government has reaffirmed what we can do – Stay at home, Protect the NHS, Save lives. So do that. But also, as my friend Josie says, all we can do is give what we have in our hands. The best thing to do is not wish that you were someone else with a more useful gift but just to be who you were made to be and give what you can. Peace.]

Gratitude #39

We haven't even left the garden today,
but I watched the clouds sail across the sky.
Strange and lonely, isn't it, this time?
I find myself thinking, is everyone else really doing this too?
Or is it just us in lonely Shropshire?
The children are in holiday mode,
which means they spend most of the day watching TV
or running around the garden.
Annie is delighted with so much entertainment.
And in the meantime, we move a fridge and clean the gerbil cage.
Thankful for my husband who is doing jobs all day,
while I look after Annie and make lunch and lemon cake.
It doesn't feel like the Easter holidays,
it doesn't feel like anything much except for quietness, a breath.
We made no plans for this year,
we just said let's get into the house and then see.
And now everything has been wiped clean it seems, a blank slate.
What does this mean for us all I wonder?
I feel too tired to be learning anything, but I'm sure I am, deep down.

04.04.20

Gratitude #40

We plan to make a list of everything we see out on our walk today.
At the end of the lane, Sam already has a ladybird on his cap.
We turn left and a rabbit hops out in front of us,
turn along the footpath and see a red admiral on a leaf.
We can hear the bleating of lambs.
There are birds swooping over us as we walk in the sun.
We forget to count any more.
Back home, I lie on the trampoline, letting it take the weight of me.
I can see another cherry tree, to make up for the one we left behind,
and a bush that looks like fire, its red buds beginning to unfurl.
The leaves and buds frame my view of the sky,
and I think I could lie here like this all summer.
It feels like rest.
This house and its garden feel like rest,
even though we are run ragged with the children,
who are fighting and missing their friends.
We are feeling our way into the landscape, into this place,
gathering it into us, somehow, anchoring ourselves to it somehow.

05.04.20

Gratitude #41

Thankful for family, their little faces on screens,
Ben running around with his friend on FaceTime, showing him
drawings.
Sam settles into happiness today with origami and baking.
Ivy finally finishes her room and finds a home for everything.
The rest of the house, however, remains unfinished.
We don't leave the garden today, and thinking back,
I can't even remember what we did.
Time gets broken up into tiny blocks with children;
we baked, and we did craft, then Annie napped and we ate lunch,
and it is all the little things like this that run from one to the other,
that sew up our days, that are nothing and everything,
focusing on the little things, like children do.
This is how we get though today;
hiding out with the nation
until this is all over.
Please can this soon be all over?

06.04.20

Gratitude #42

Thankful for a lie in, and then breakfast in bed,
for new coat hooks in the hallway,
for cousins who FaceTime with the children.
For finding a book that I've been wanting to read,
and for snatched hellos over the fence,
as a friend drops off gerbil food.
We go back to the old house to get some garden things;
a slide, some plants, and, seeing it's trampled upon state,
we are thankful that we have a new garden,
that we managed to get out before all the house moves stopped.
Strange to be back in that place
that had been our safety and shelter for so long,
Without all our things in it, though, it has lost its power somehow.
It feels innocent, unknown, not ours anymore.
The children say, 'I like this house' as we wander around the empty
rooms,
but they are blessed and they know it, to come back to this high up
place.
So thankful for this new house today,
that we know we can rest in, stay in, grow old in.

07.04.20

Gratitude #43

Sam and I take hold of Annie's hands, one each,
and walk in the hot, hot sun down the lane.
She throws each leg out with unbent knees,
with jerky, foreign movements.
It is as hot as the hottest summer day,
and we could all close our eyes, pretend that this wasn't happening.
It is quiet, and I long for the food to last for weeks,
so I don't have to go out, to face the sad realities of life.
We walk slowly down the dusty track to the bridge
and look at the field of lambs on either side of the road.
Annie points at them, in all their newness and whiteness.
Sam says, 'Can we do this again, go for a walk, just us?'
And I think it is magical how the simplest, the plainest of things
are the things that they want to do again.
I swear as parents we sometimes want to do
more and more and more for our children,
but maybe what they need is less and less and less.
Until there is just us, standing by a field and talking,
holding hands with our sweet girl,
leading her back up the lane.

08.04.20

Gratitude #44

I am meant to be cleaning but how can I not write
when I am in communion with this house?
We are alone for the first time in weeks.
It almost makes me want to cry.
All the things that have happened here come back to my mind.
I got a book published, I had a baby,
Ivy had a diagnosis that would change her life and ours.
My husband made three albums here.
These rooms have held us, all of us for six years.
All of our tears and laughter, all of our secrets and sorrows.
This house reminds me of writing,
because I found myself here as a writer, in its shade and solitude.
Sleepy wasps crawled out of the floorboards here,
a bat flew in and made his home in the bathroom for a few weeks,
a bunny got dragged in by the cat
and made its way down to the lounge, hopping about.
Such stories it has held.
It is old and tired but also wooden and warm.
And it holds me now as it has for six years.
And yes there have always been compromises;
the landlord who wouldn't redecorate but also never put the rent up,
the way that we could never quite settle
because we knew that we would be moving on.
But this house leaves peace with me now,
after the sorrows and mountains climbed.
It feels like this old house is my friend today,
the one who knew me best in this village.
All my rhythms, my reasons.
He knows all my secrets and will carry them with him,
in his old wooden heart,
and just as we never knew the secrets

of the ones who came before us (though I often wondered),
he won't tell mine either.
And so there is an understanding between us, old friend.
And I say peace to whoever comes here next,
peace and the unfolding of dreams.

09.04.20

Gratitude #45

How do you write a love song when you don't know where to start?
When you can't see black from white because all the lines are blurred?
They say you don't know what you've got til it's gone
but this virus and the stories you hear
make you see what you have and hold it in your hands.
I want to know you and be thankful for you every day of my life.
We were young when we first met and didn't know quite who we
were.
We grew up together and still saw eye to eye at the end of it.
I see the ways you love me; the lie-ins, the cups of tea, the support,
the talking, always the talking, through our worries and out the other
side again,
the praying; looking upwards together for guidance as we walk this
road.
This is the day too, that the world mourned for what it thought it had
lost,
the beauty that lived right among it, down here with the needy and
lovesick ones.
It mourned him, thought all hope was gone, but it didn't know what
was coming,
what light was breaking through.

10.04.20

(Note: Good Friday)

Gratitude #46

Thankful for Annie, giggling into my cheek at 8.30pm
when she is supposed to be asleep.
Thankful for this warm sun that feels like a blessing to the earth,
even though this pandemic rages on.
Thankful for virtual catch ups and tiny faces in phone screens,
even though the sound is awful,
and the delay makes it impossible to have a conversation.
At least we can look at each other's faces,
and pretend that everything is normal.
Thankful for good news.
Easter Saturday is the day of waiting,
the day of breath-held expectation.
Well that's how we see it now, in retrospect.
But at the time, it was a dark day,
of disappointment, of bewildering grief.
And today is like that for some; they are groping around
in the dark for hope.
And for some it will take a long time to see the glimmer of light
breaking through.
It will take a long time to believe again in goodness, to trust in
laughter.

But humanity's gift is this old earth, spinning on,
with enough joy in each day to last for a lifetime,
with enough beauty to keep us full to the brim with thankfulness.

If you want to be full, look at the clouds,
look into the eyes of others,
look at the ferns, the birds, the sunset.
Look and then keep looking for as long as you are alive.

11.04.20

[I just love spring. I struggle in winter, with creativity and being cold and feeling hopeless, but am just in love with how quickly spring comes and then there is new life and abundance everywhere. This year has been so strange with all these things mixed up together; the glorious sun, the joy of spring, this horrendous virus sweeping the globe, and then Easter, this most amazing story of love and new life, of disappointment and despair which turned to joy and amazement.]

Gratitude #47

A quiet day, where there is space to think.
The children hunt for treasure in the garden
and we eat roast beef for lunch.
We wander down to the lambs again.
Now the children are watching Indiana Jones
and I am sitting here with you my sweet love,
feeding you tea slowly and quietly,
just like we used to before life changed.
More and more I am thinking about how we will get back to normal,
or learn to live long term with this new normal,
and how I will be able to write again.
I am remembering how delightful it is to watch you emerge,
as you say 'baa' and lead me to the gate,
as you lead me around the garden
and I follow where you want to go,
as you start to sing a song to yourself and I join in.

12.4.20

Gratitude #48

I scrub the doors,
erasing years of evidence of your heights, your unformed handwriting.
I have always thought it amazing how these things around us
bear the marks of our history, and we pass through, ethereal, ghostly.
We leave no sense of ourselves, just the photographs we take,
the things we write, the things we do, if there is someone to tell about
them.
But this old house bears the scars of our having been here.
I think of you, dear Sam when we first moved in.
Three years old, glue ear, a speech impediment
and now in this short chapter you are suddenly ten!
Lanky and skinny, loving stats and football.
Missing your friends, but finding things to do:
ticking off the activities your school has sent;
origami flowers, an Easter garden, painting, baking.
I don't know where that other boy went.
I miss him, and his 'Nook, nook Mummy!'
when he was about to do something good.
I thought I had the measure of him, but not you.
You are already better at maths than me,
probably know more about nature and
definitely know more about football than I do.
You are a pool of deep water,
a world of mysteries that I have not plumbed the depths of.
Thankful today for the boy you were,
the boy you are, the person you are becoming.

13.04.20

Gratitude #49

The A49, normally so full
of fight or flight,
is now a pale empty ribbon
glinting in the sunlight.
Our lives, once so jam-packed
that there was no time to think,
have been emptied out too.

And what does it feel like now?
Stripped back and bare, empty but still full.

Perhaps we are learning again,
how to be at peace,
how to pace ourselves,
how to conserve our strength,
how to keep going,
one day at a time.

14.04.20

*[Looked out of the window today and saw the A49 all pale and silent, completely empty.
I am thankful for the 'big pause' as I heard it described today, but there are also
challenges of being at home with four children, I'm not gonna lie! It is very demanding in
terms of time and for some reason they think it's acceptable to stay up til 9pm! I crave
time to myself just to sit still, drink tea, eat chocolate and have a few thoughts to myself.
So although everything has stopped, there is still parenting! We are nearly finished on the
old house and meanwhile we are still trying to get jobs done whilst looking after little
people and not being able to buy anything very easily. We'll get there!]*

Gratitude #50

My heart has had enough today of staying away from everyone,
of biding our time.
But it is one of those times where you can't do anything
to change the way things are.
All you can control is your state of mind.
And some days, and sometimes it takes a lot of effort
to empty your mind of worries, to still yourself, to breathe in slowly,
to be thankful for this moment,
even though we do not know what is coming
or what tomorrow will look like.
Today I am thankful that there are some choices left
and that this is one of them.

15.04.20

*[It feels hard today and I feel a bit tetchy. So I'm just having five minutes on my bench.
Thankful that I get this amazing view to look at. And thankful for realising that I feel
stressed today and taking time to do a little bit of deep breathing. We can't change this
situation, all we can do is look after our mental, physical and emotional health while
going through it. Hope you're all doing ok today.]*

Gratitude #51

Today I make lunch as bright as possible,
pile up lettuce, olives, beetroot, avocado,
tomatoes, cucumber and halloumi and cover it all with dressing.
It is all the freshness and goodness that I need today.
The kids run feral in the garden, making dens in the bushes
while I put up the pictures for my family photo wall.
Today is a day for deciding where the art goes and its confusing.
We're not sure if any of this art suits us anymore.
We wonder if art is about the house or the person.
We can't decide what to put where
and so, we leave them stacked up against the walls all day,
hoping that some decisions might make themselves.
We still feel half here, still moving things around, not fully settled.
We'll get there soon though,
will find a rhythm in all this open-ended madness.

16.04.20

Gratitude #52

Learning today from the wisdom of the trees.
There is a young tree standing on its own, in a clearing,
perfectly symmetrical
because it has the space to expand in any way it wants to.
I wonder what can grow in us now that the big pause
has cleared the land around us.
The second is a group of branches, gathered low at the stem.
They sway in the wind and I think if they didn't move,
they would crack.
Their strength is in their ability to bend and swerve, to flex and shift.
And I wonder if our roots are being strengthened
as we adapt to this new way of being.
The third tree was felled by a storm, hollowed out at its core,
and from its carcass new growth shoots up,
not a thin shoot but a strong new branch with flawless, youthful bark.
And I wonder what will come from the carcass of this year?
Something stronger, resilient, a vivid shoot of green?

17.04.20

*[The wisdom of the trees. We went to the woods today for a walk. It was good to do
something different and we all enjoyed the fresh air in our lungs.]*

Gratitude #53

Thankful for home where I can rest and be myself.
Home where it is warm, though the storm rages outside.
Home where everything is just as I need it, all my books, my loves,
Ivy's jelly babies, Annie's milk. Biscuits. Teabags.
Everything that we need to get through.
Thinking of what 'home' used to mean too:
that certain, specific smell that you would find nowhere else.
Apples, mixed with books, mixed with diesel and craft glue.
All the things that went on there; the fixing, the cooking, the reading,
the life as usual: busy, messy and chaotic but safe.
A home from home where we can't go just now,
where we will be together again soon.
But for now, there is this nest, these children, changing, racing
through their lives, growing, growing, growing.
And us too, and this garden.
The children's clothes are getting too small,
and the laptop that holds all my thoughts is dying on me.
There is no standing still.
But in all this racing and growing,
there is still time to rest, to write, to ponder.
You've seen the athletes race. Everyone runs; one wins. Run to win.
Is there something holy in this running I wonder?
Something of rest in the running?

18.04.20

[Thankful for home today. Am setting up a desk slowly, slowly, slowly (after already shifting it once). It will have to be in the lounge for now but the view is bliss. I should add that because Ivy is T1 diabetic, jelly babies are her lifeline. I never feel relaxed without a few packs in the cupboard!]

Gratitude #54

A walk in the wilderness
where one tree leans on another.
The way Annie pauses to watch the 'baas'.
A long talk with a good friend on the phone,
with a G+T in one hand, whilst following Annie around the garden.
A socially distanced chat with our new neighbour
and her daughter over the fence.
The way that the field glows at dusk.
I see it in passing while I am making Annie's bottle
and it is bright and fiery
and takes my breath away.

19.04.20

Gratitude #55

For two hours to write and read,
to plunge back into things
that I have left untouched for weeks.
For the sun which lends its kindness
to us again.
For the children, who like the
structure of home-school,
and who luxuriate in the
warmth of the garden afterwards.
For a meal that everyone eats without complaint, for once.
Okay so it's only pasta with tomato sauce but it's a start.

20.04.20

Gratitude #56

Thankful for that moment of quiet,
walking through the garden
when the children were all inside,
where the sky was beginning to dull
and the sheep were still calling.
For dinner with my husband
even though the baby came to join us
because she couldn't get to sleep in the light.
Right now, hope doesn't look like
the hope we're used to;
the knowing and ticking off of days.
It doesn't look like an arrow
with a fixed mark ahead of it.
We don't know what is coming tomorrow,
or how long this will go on for.
And hope has become more like
a thread that we cling to,
that one day soon this will all be over,
that one day soon we will be able
to hug our parents,
that one day soon there will be a vaccine.

21.04.20

Gratitude #57

I turn to see the bright field
at dusk,
in the inky blue of bedtime,
and then first thing
in the morning,
where it glows against the
warming sky like a beacon
or a flash of hope.

It is a new day.

22.04.20

[Another day, another poem. Today's poem is a little ode to 'The Bright Field' by RS Thomas, all about our own bright field. Hope you are all managing, whatever your situation is at this strange time. Today is a new day. And if today didn't go so well, tomorrow is another! Taking it one day at a time helps me when I'm feeling overwhelmed / stuck / depressed / trapped at home!]

Gratitude #58

Does anybody else feel that we have skipped a season,
which is adding to the general sense of displacement?
We are out of place but firmly in our place - at home.
I started writing to get me through the dregs of winter,
and now, 58 posts in, it feels like full summer,
the kids running around the garden barefoot,
with the light evenings and their tireless chatter at bedtime.
We have missed spring, it seems, and how I love spring;
its precious unfurling, each bud exploding open like a gift,
the surprise of each good day, as they are not a given in spring.
I have missed the quiet awakening of creativity, too, this year.
I always feel like writing at this time; there is room to unfold
and find oneself after the making do of winter.
It is the time to get your hands back, after winter's cruelty,
and get your dreams back out of their box after hibernation.
Where are the spring rains this year I wonder?
I can't wait to see the rain in this house,
from this view that will be my constant, now.
I can't wait to see a storm come in over the hills.
But the great surprise this year is that here we are,
away in our own little world together,
enjoying the youth of spring every day,
all the newness of the world,
the kindness of the sun in the mornings.
We have this spring more than we have ever had a spring,
together as a family, but at the same time, I miss it,
and feel it has been taken from me somehow.
They should call it the awakening, shouldn't they?
Of the sleeping earth, of all the dreams that lie dormant.
And then I realise that spring hasn't been taken from me,
but shared with those that I love.

And sharing is good, and always to be treasured.
And perhaps those things in me, in all of us, are still waking up.
Perhaps, this year, this strangest of all years,
will make us see them in all clarity for what they really are.
It is the being taken 'out of' that we notice.
The being plucked from what is normal and planted here,
here where we know, but in a way that we don't know.
Maybe this year will lend us a vision that we have never had before.

23.04.20

Gratitude #59

Dear birds,
please be our healers,
our message bringers,
our sweet talkers.
Whether we be city dwellers
or country folk,
you birds are the only ones
who can visit us all.
Whether we have lost our best friend,
or are tethered to our home,
whether we are lonely or overcrowded,
may your gentle 'per-wit',
your 'chee-chee',
your slow 'coo-coo'
be a balm to our souls.
May we sleep like birds of the air
who know they have a nest.
May we wake in the morning
like sparrows who know
that they are cared for.
And wherever we are,
may we find an open window
and listen.

24.04.20

[We found ourselves in a particularly chatty bird area on our walk so I recorded it and then I just got the poem just now, after dinner, all in one sentence almost. It has been a tricky day today, with frayed tempers and an overcrowded house but the birds are always a balm to me and I hope to you too. Peace, everybody.]

Gratitude #60

I start out with a visit to Sainsbury's
and am thankful for these friendly workers,
the ones I have seen for years going about their day
with laughter and smiles.
It feels strange to be out in the world,
with people queuing to get in the shop
but inside I feel kind of normal
until someone walks past wearing some kind of a mask.
And then I remember why we are all doing this.
I buy as much as I can fit in the trolley
 and come home to a barrage of questions,
dramas, tears and laughter.
There aren't many moments to reflect today,
just this one, now, sitting in the kitchen,
having just finished a mountain of washing up,
the spotlights reflected in the black window pane,
the fridge humming away behind me.
I am thankful today for hand painted new home cards,
and cards with beautiful words,
thankful for little windfalls and surprises.
Thankful for sunflower seeds to plant.
It takes a while for my heart to slow right down
after the children have gone to bed.
And then by the time I get there, later, I can't sleep
and lie awake wondering about things.
Like why are all these people dying
and what can we do to stop it
and what shall we have for lunch tomorrow
and why can't I get any work done
and why do I get so angry with the kids.
But there is grace and there is time.

The things will all get done.
So, I will hold my peace.
I will make it a part of me
and let it not depart from me.

25.04.20

Gratitude #61

The first moody skies, the first rains.
They lift the scent of all these plants
that we don't yet know the names of.
The boys play football all afternoon
and we wander about, potter and dream.
We see the already planned, -
the careful choices
of the one who lived here last.
We wonder what to do first,
whether to wait for the blooms
this year and make changes later.
For the first time,
we don't have to rush,
and we aren't making do.
We can watch it all unfurl,
choose, change our minds,
edit as we go, change as we grow,
put our roots way down deep.

26.04.20

Gratitude #62

It has been hard today,
we're all tired of being cooped up,
of having to juggle sorting the house
with home-school with admin with work
and sometimes it's just too much.
But there are still jewels there,
hiding beneath the rage or the tiredness.
We watch Annie trying to stand, and clap
her as she balances for a few seconds,
her mouth opened in an o,
impressed with herself.
I cook one of my favourite dinners tonight;
a cobbled together chicken salad,
with roasted veg and couscous, feta, olives and flatbreads.
The children make faces and mostly eat bread and chicken.
To finish we have Ben's amazing scones with fig jam and whipped
cream.
One of the best things about this lockdown
is the enforced dinner eating.
Not that it is an enjoyable occasion,
rather it is messy, noisy, and hectic.
But we know that we will all eat together,
every night so we are making things
that we haven't had in ages,
or that the kids have never tried before.
The children eventually screech their way into bed
and I sit down, in stony silence
to revive myself with another cup of tea.
At least I will be worn out with life when I am done here.
Every time I see a bad photo of myself,
looking older than I think I should,

I think of that amazing quote by George Bernard Shaw:
'This is the true joy in life, the being used for a purpose
recognised by yourself as a mighty one;
the being thoroughly worn out
before you are thrown on the scrap heap'.
I am that. Worn out and happy.

27.04.20

Gratitude #63

Was it the snatched moments of quiet at breakfast time,
when the others had not quite woken?
or was it watching my three big loons dance around after dinner,
dressed as superheroes?
Was it the minutes that I spent watching you fall asleep, dear one,
twirling your dummy and then succumbing, finally, to rest?
Or is it this moment now, of shared communion
with these listeners around the globe,
as the strings and layers of Tiny Leaves filter down
through iPhone screens and into lounges?
There are many things, and who knows which is the most precious
or if it would be wise to say.
I haven't talked about the things that left me sad, tired or angry today,
but they came, too.
But like Ada Limon said, there is something defiant, isn't there,
in joyful living? In painful living?
In all of it, this glorious mess that we make each day of our lives.
And something in me wants to rise up
when things are hard or good,
or both in equal measure and say,
like she says, like the trees say,
'Fine then, I'll take it all.'

28.04.20

[I love this thought that when the bad stuff comes, we would stand there like a tree and just be like, 'I'll take it!' This life is so gloriously complicated and messy and wonderful all at the same time.]

(Note: The last line is borrowed from 'Instructions on Not Giving Up' by Ada Limon. It's really good - look it up!)

Gratitude #64

This is the thing that makes
me feel most at home.
I have unpacked my desk finally,
put all my books on the shelf,
gathered all my pens and post-its,
plugged in my lamp and
now it casts a warm glow over the desk.
As always, today has been impossible,
a baby crawling around and eating everything,
three children in different years needing different support
that I can't give all at the same time,
especially as they all need a laptop.
So I get stressed and then they give up
and then Annie sleeps
and it is all a little easier.
After lunch, finally, the sun comes out again
and the clouds look magical.
And tonight, finally, I am finding my peace again,
finding myself again, under all these books,
these bits of paper, these pens.

29.04.20

Gratitude #65

Quick! I have found a second!
As soon as Annie naps
I leave the children with Joel
(they are writing a play),
and I plug in my earphones and write.
In this pandemic, which looks quiet
rather than loud, lonely rather than populated,
I zone out of my house and try to remember
what I was writing before all this happened.

What will come from this I wonder?
And I think of it the way I see my life,
that we are sometimes too close in to the things
that we are learning for them to make sense to us.
It is only in retrospect, in looking backwards,
that we see how it has shaped and changed
the river of our life,
why we did this or that afterwards,
the imprint it made on our lives.

30.04.20

Gratitude #66

A late morning,
a prayer.
I help the boys with their work
and we get a little bit done.
After lunch we walk
through the sheep field in the rain.
These days are beginning to
look awfully similar,
but there is some difference
in their sameness.
Different conversations,
different thoughts.
Tonight we watch a documentary
about Icelandic music
and, for a while,
we are somewhere else entirely.

01.05.20

Gratitude #67

For this new world in which a Tory minister
stands up and says that 90% of known rough sleepers
have been offered a bed and are staying in hotels
or other safe places.
For a world in which the lonely are being looked after,
shielded, bought food packages.
For a world where someone suffering domestic abuse
can walk into Boots and say 'I need help'.
For a world which knows
that it is the critical workers
that keep this world ticking over.
For the life savers.
Who knew that along with the grief,
this virus could flick the switch from money making to love?
Could put the most needy at the top of the political agenda?
What was it that Boris said?
'The NHS is the beating heart of this country.'
Keep us in this place where compassion and love
are the things we strive for, where justice and righteousness
are the values we uphold above all.
Our country is built on making do, putting up with,
that stoic sense of humour but also love.
The carers, the befrienders, the teachers, the social workers,
the hands and heart of this place.
Where staying in is the new going out,
we have had conversation upon conversation
with the children in which we make sense of this world,
discussing things that we didn't have time to talk about before,
the way that we used to spend time as adolescents
at my parents table, the constant stream of babble
a soothing chaos as we made sense of the world.

02.05.20

(Note: I think I'm a bit naïve sometimes. Especially when it comes to trusting MPs.)

Gratitude #68

Went to church online today,
then made a lasagne for lunch.
I haven't made a lasagne in years
as I never have the time.
It was delicious even though
the boys refused to eat it.
It has been one of those days
where you fill your time with doodles,
videos and Whatsapps with family,
who set challenges for the kids
to keep them entertained.
Sam tries to learn backflips
and Ben 'tries his hardest' at football,
coming back in bright red and sweating.
It is one of those days
where the morning slides into lunch,
which slides into dinner and then already,
the littlest is rubbing her eyes for bedtime.
Tonight we catch up with two of my favourites
on FaceTime who we will hang out with
as soon as this is all over.

03.05.20

Gratitude #69

All about 139,
in which there is a radical love song.
I read it today and am reminded,
and carried up out of this place.
For what else are we looking for
but to be known?
And what else are we longing for
but to be loved?
From the time I wake up in the morning,
there you are.
Every day, no matter how tired,
how worn ragged I am, there you are.
And when I lay my head down,
there you are.

04.05.20

(Note: this one is about Psalm 139.)

Gratitude #70

For the gentle peep peep
of the train that passes
at the back of the house.
It makes me feel connected
in all this aloneness.
At night, its lit-up windows
are a streamer of light
across the darkness.
For the 'baas' of the sheep
in the field down the hill
that make me feel grounded
in all this aloneness,
pinned to the earth.
For the crows calling,
for the warm wind
that rustles the leaves, and says ssh,
still yourself, all will be well.
For all the normal, glorious things
that happen each day
and go on happening.

05.05.20

Gratitude #71

The full moon, glowing at dusk,
and the audacious song thrush
calling out from his tree,
so small but yet so loud!
He calls, repeats,
waits and calls again.
It makes me wonder how
loud our songs are heard
and how far they spread
beyond our knowing.

06.05.20

Gratitude #72

The way they are all leaning over,
straining towards the light,
drinking it in as they know
it is what they need.
The way they turn themselves
to stay loved by the sun,
just that little bit longer.
And I thought today that
no one can argue
with a love story, no one can say
it isn't real or it didn't happen,
because it is the very roots of you,
the very you of you,
just like these seedlings
who know what they need,
and reach towards it.

07.05.20

[Just look at these little seedlings, gift from a dear friend, teaching me how to live. Reaching for what they know they need.]

Gratitude #73

Seems so strange
that half a lifetime ago
the lights were all turned out,
the young men had gone off to fight, and
the children had been sent away.
And this nation just kept on,
believing they were doing the right thing.
All that, for us, for freedom,
and we sit here toasting our thanks
to them with Prosecco and cake,
75 years later.

08.05.20

(Note: 75th anniversary of VE Day)

Gratitude #74

Cutting down
the conifer
on a hot day.
I turn the corner
of the house,
after emptying
the wheelbarrow
and my heart sings-
the hills!

09.05.20

Gratitude #75

We walk outside to the terrace
with steaming cups of tea.
The birdsong wraps around us;
it circles and rains down,
among the leaves rustling,
the sudden chill.
The children make stained glass windows
and felt creatures.
Sam makes lemon posset lollies
and we watch the Jungle Book.
Ben makes us all cards with pop up initials.
He is sad when Boris says
he might have to go back to school first
and we see the end of the tunnel,
and maybe we don't want to see it yet.
After all of this,
I'm not sure I'm ready to emerge.
It is a good day, full of tiny smiles,
fights, prayers and laughter.

10.05.20

Gratitude #76

Feel today like I am a cupboard
that is almost bare.
We are carefully living on the remnants
but whatever little is there,
the children ransack shamelessly;
my patience,
my time,
my energy.
If they weren't here,
I'd be writing, working, thinking,
but instead I am spending all my time
tidying up or arguing with them,
trying to bribe them into doing
work that they don't want to do.
I find time to make a lemon cake though
(with no helpers) and Joel cooks me dinner.
It's nearly bedtime
and then I will have a few hours of peace,
and for that I am thankful.

11.05.20

Gratitude #77

Was it the high track along the ridgeback,
not another human in sight?
Was it the birds circling as we walked,
calling and swooping down, as if looking for carrion?
Was it the clouds lighting up the shapes of these hills
that we know and love, that we now call our home?
Or the wind lifting our hair away from our faces,
the children running ahead of us, as wild as ever, Annie
chatting into the wind?
Who can say what I am most thankful for, what is the most
important, what I will remember?
(Except for one thing, a small and wondrous thing- good news from a
friend.)
I've always loved this hill, the way it sets one path before you,
and says choose this, there is no other way,
just this one will take you there.

12.05.20

(Note: We were walking on the Lawley, one of my favourite hills. The 'small and wondrous thing' was the safe delivery of the baby of a dear friend I'd been texting just hours before!)

Gratitude #78

There is a pink tinge to the sky,
a warm glow that lifts the grey.
Up close there is the dry stalk of a tree
that looks dead but is not.
There is the flat crown of a cherry tree
that spreads itself under the cable.
There are the ridged tiles of the house
in front, and, beyond that,
a patchwork of fields,
pinky-brown, yellow-green, fresh green.
There are clouds of trees,
and beyond them,
the volcanic fault line, dark green,
glowing with swathes of burnt orange.
Up close, I know it is last years' bracken,
crumpled and dried out like paper,
up close I know it is being reborn already
as the young shoots push through,
curl their way up into life.
The children are in bed,
I have made my strong and sweet tea,
and I settle down to work.
But first. Rest, look, be restored.

13.05.20

(Note: this poem was an attempt at capturing everything I could see from my window at that moment in time.)

Gratitude #79

We don't go out for a walk today.
Instead we potter in the garden
as the weather is kind.
We begin many jobs
that we probably won't get around
to finishing for ages because it is dinner time,
or the baby has crawled off,
or because we need some help
from a handy dad,
and they can't come around right now.
You release the apple tree
from its entanglement in the holly
and I walk about the place with Annie
and dream about what we can do
in all of these spaces.

14.05.20

Gratitude #80

These new fronds curl up,
strong-necked,
out of the dark earth,
out of the cracked debris
of their former self,

and begin to unfurl.

15.05.20

Gratitude #81

A walk up in a high place today
where there is grass that is smooth
under foot.
We can see a long way in every direction.
It is good to be up here,
out of the way,
out of our house for a while.

16.05.20

(Note: a walk at Mitchell's Fold).

Gratitude #82

Today I wake to the sound of birdsong.
It is a cloak of joy around me
and I remember how Annie
is always happy when she wakes.
It reminds me to be the same.
We have a coffee in the garden
while the children play.
We make roast chicken for lunch
with lemon, garlic and thyme.
It is one of those days
where the day is sliced in two,
where you don't understand
how this is going to go away,
or how we will ever get through this,
where you miss your parents,
your family, your friends.
But at the same time you realise
that finding the little things
and naming them
will hold you up from day to day.

17.05.20

(Note: I also wrote this today, not as a thankfulness poem but a kind of grieving for lost work...

*A note to all the creatives
who cannot hear their own thoughts.
Who cannot produce work
because they cannot hear,
who cannot hear because*

there is no time that is not
filled to the brim with voices.
I want to say and I want it to be true
that your work is not lost,
that your poems are not
escaping through your fingers,
running away from you.
I have said that before,
but it is different this time,
because all of us are trying
to make sense of this,
in this time where we have
all the time and no time.
They will come back at the right time
if you have eyes that are open,
if you have ears for hearing,
if you are willing to go a little slower
than you normally would have.)

Gratitude #83

Today I am thankful for the most delicious cake I have ever tasted -
a gift from my sister in law for my birthday tomorrow.
I am thankful for the warm breeze today
and the scent of the Mexican orange blossom in the garden.
I am thankful for time at the football field in the afternoon
where the boys practice shots, Ivy practises her leaps
and Annie tries to put step after step together.

18.05.20

Gratitude #84

I am humbled by all the love
that flies down the internet,
and onto the doorstep today.
The phone starts pinging in the morning
and there is a pile of gifts to unwrap.
There are deliveries through the day,
each one a wonderful surprise.
It is warm and breezy today
and everything feels just right.
We make French toast for lunch
with bananas, blueberries and bacon,
washed down with Buck's Fizz.
I'm humbled to be thought of
and loved today, shown love by every
message, gift and card.
My children make cards with my favourite things:
birds, ferns, a picture of a holiday to Greece
that we dream of taking when this is all done.
Thankful today, just to be me,
to have this band of love around me.

19.05.20

Gratitude #85

Inside it is messy
and there are so many people
living all of their hours in this space
that it is hard to keep on top of everything.

I step outside
and the sky is huge and bare,
the light on the hills is just right,
the cool breeze on my skin
is like a cup of cold water to the soul.
I can hear a field full of sheep calling
and the gentle strains of a piano
from behind a closed door.
There is all the time in the world,
it seems,
all the space in the world.

20.05.20

Gratitude #86

In the morning, the kids tick off their tasks, whilst Annie crawls
around unplugging their laptops, shutting her fingers in drawers
and scribbling in their books.
I take her out for a walk around the garden when she (and they) have
had enough.
I look up and notice how the field is crumpled up like a blanket,
how the light casts its shadows across it, which change through the
day.

I am selfish with my time and the minute I put Annie down for her
nap I start work. I get a solid two hours work done which feels good.

The rest of the day is a mess of tears, painful toes, and arguments.
And then we find a DVD we made of the first five years with the kids.
The nostalgia fills the kids when they watch it. And it looks like it was
all smiles, it's true. But it was hard too, like every other day is. But
when we tell the stories, we think mostly of the good.

Like now, when we could choose to tell
of deprivation or bounty
depending on how we look at it.

21.05.20

Gratitude #87

Today has slipped
through my fingers, somehow.
It has got away from me before
I have had a chance to do
anything useful with it.
How many days are like this now?
The wind whips the long grass
into a fury in the field.
The ash tree shakes itself
mournfully outside the window.
See how nature itself is fast and slow,
yet we do not count the grass
more worthy than the tree.
Going fast is not everything.
And so today is everything and nothing,
just as every other day is.

22.05.20

Gratitude #88

I have felt better today.
Maybe it is because the pressure is off.
No more home-school for a week.
The children have new books to explore
and a list of things they want to do
so they are happy.
Annie falls asleep snuggling
with her big sister in the hammock,
even though the wind is running over this hill,
rustling the leaves above their heads.
While she sleeps
we sort out the greenhouse,
throwing away bags of random bits of string
and five-year-old seeds.
We take a van load of conifer to the tip.
It is all sorts of normal
but it feels lighter somehow.

23.05.20

Gratitude #89

Is it ok that I am tired now?
I'm tired of the voices all the time,
of the excitement and noise
rising at bedtime,
when we're like 'No, no, it's bedtime,
we need some time to ourselves',
and for a long time I can still hear
the bubble of their voices
along the corridor.

I look outside
at the lovely old hills,
still glowing in the evening light.
Still, alive, constant.
They have been here for 560 million years
so they know a thing or two about
waiting,
being at peace,
rest.

24.05.20

Gratitude #90

The birds call me from sleeping to living, Joel brings me a cup of tea
and our little daughter calls 'mama' from the doorway.
You just can't wake in a bad mood with a one-year-old.
These days are tumbling one into the other,
with no thought for order, time, routine.
How will we ever get back to living normally?
We try to grab hold of one or two hours work each a day,
just so that we don't go insane.
The children start by drawing,
then go outside to play football and make dens.
The sprinkler comes out to try to save the already straw-like lawn.
Later, for twenty blissful minutes,
I read a new poetry book in the hammock.
Meanwhile, in the real world, the whole country boils with anger
at those who think the rules don't apply to them,
even though they made the rules.
It doesn't feel like a bank holiday, who knows what it feels like;
some hot, nameless, beautiful day
in this strange, unending year.

25.05.20

Gratitude #91

There is not the togetherness that you might feel,
walking through a London park or down a sunny high street,
where the presence of others confirms in some way
that you are right to be spending your time like this.
I felt like that often living in the South East,
I liked feeling part of something bigger than myself.

But up here instead there is this hush, this shared secret;
it is empty and beautiful.
It feels that you are walking among the clouds up here,
in a secret, heavenly place.

26.05.20

[Note: a walk on the Ragleth.]

Gratitude #92

It seems so much like all of this
is about rest:
the being in one place,
the undoing of all that is normal.

I stubbornly plough on with work
while Annie naps,
diving desperately down for jewels,
like a starving kingfisher.

Later, she drinks her milk
in the hammock
and I listen to the others
shrieking with delight, a way off.
I realise I must claim this minute,
this stillness,
because otherwise it will be gone.

And after everything, the silver birches
are all soft and forgiveness and grace,
each day of this unassuming year.

27.05.20

Gratitude #93

Sometimes
it is as simple
as the pop
of a strawberry
in your mouth;
the way it hurts
as it dissolves
on your tongue,
the tang of
dizzying sweetness
in your throat,
the smell
on your fingers
of early summer.

28.05.20

Gratitude #94

The sun beats down on us
and we retreat to the
leafy shade for our first barbeque
at the new house.
The Wrekin is on fire tonight,
strange creature:
where once its belly burned with fire,
it now rages upon its grassy back.
All the fire and all the life.
While this pandemic rages
like fire over the world
all the small miracles are still happening,
new life comes into the world,
all the flowers bloom,
these children come into being.

29.05.20

(Note: we had news of another precious baby born today)

Gratitude #95

Even though he is now six,
he still has a little heart inside of him,
and in the scorching sun we get out planks of wood
to make a ramp down the steps for his hot wheels.
He shows his baby sister the joy of cars
and she squeals with delight as she watches them go
and then puts one on the track herself.
When he was at preschool,
I would buy him a new car every few weeks,
in return for good behaviour at the supermarket.
It was my love letter to him in metal and paint,
and even now, big boy, little boy,
he pulls out his drawer, crammed full of cars,
and searches among them for the one he is looking for,
turns it around in his hands,
says 'this is my best, he's the fastest'.

30.05.20

Gratitude #96

It had to do with the hour after lunch
where I snuck back into bed
under the pretence
of getting the baby to sleep,
and I turned and picked up
'The Hiding Place' by Corrie Ten Boom,
and I was transported again
to the prison camp,
to the dorms of women,
to the life she lived.
I can't believe what she faced,
and how she lived through it
with such grace.
And I think if I were to face such a trial,
what would I do, and would I have strength
enough to stand up under it?
Would love shine through,
despite it all, in the midst of all?

31.05.20

Gratitude #97

And so the world opens its doors and slowly people start to go outside,
to meet with others, cautiously, to move in small circles.
And meanwhile the world is on fire at this injustice,
and deservedly so.
How long will it be until all of us live as one,
until we see each other as one?
Until every life weighs the same as every other life?
I know righteous anger when I see it,
I know the sound of millions of voices calling out for justice.
Today feels like a new season but things will be strange
and different for a long time.
So I will stop here, it feels like the time,
but I won't stop being thankful for the little things,
each day left for me on this old earth
is another chance to say it.

01.06.20

[The last one. The UK is coming out of lockdown and it feels like a good time to stop writing now. Thankyou everyone for reading and for all your kind words xx]

(Note: the injustice refers to the killing of George Floyd, a 46-year-old black man, who was arrested for allegedly using a counterfeit bill. A white police officer knelt on his neck for almost eight minutes, while Floyd repeatedly said, 'I can't breathe' and begged for his life.)

Gratitude #98

Because when she crawls
she has no choice
but to get involved
with the whole business of this messy life.
She crawls along with handfuls of it,
it gets under her nails,
her cold fingers clutch the gravel.
'Do you want to hold my hand?', I ask,
and she unclutches her fist,
drops the gravel
and the rain
and the wet leaves
and takes my hand instead.
Her hand is cold
but she doesn't mind
because she is in it,
this whole messy life,
Holding it with her own two hands
on her gravelly knees,
with her wind-blown hair.

11.06.20

Gratitude #99

Because when he said, 'I can't breathe', it woke us all up from a
nightmare.

It opened our ears to our deafness, our eyes to our blindness,
it pointed out our bias where we thought that we were blameless.

And where do we go from here, now that we are blinking in the light?

We stop talking, we start reading, we say sorry, we try again.

For George Floyd and all the others that we didn't listen to.

12.06.20

Gratitude #100

Has it taken all of this stopping
to find you?
Not just this one stopping,
but stopping over and over again?
Between the fights,
on se rapproche,
they say in French;
we're getting closer.
We understand how the other
spends his or her days,
we talk more,
perhaps understand more.
Even in the closeness,
we are unfolding.

13.06.20

'Where I am folded, there I am a lie.'
        Rainer Maria Rilke, Rilke's Book of Hours: Love Poems to God